The Common Core Readiness Guide to Reading™

TIPS & TRICKS FOR
EVALUATING MULTIMEDIA CONTENT

Sandra K. Athans and Robin W. Parente

ROSEN
PUBLISHING®

New York

Published in 2015 by The Rosen Publishing Group, Inc.
29 East 21st Street, New York, NY 10010

Library of Congress Cataloging-in-Publication Data

Athans, Sandra K., 1958–
Tips & tricks for evaluating multimedia content/Sandra K. Athans and Robin W. Parente.—First Edition.
    pages cm.—(The Common Core Readiness Guide to Reading)
Includes bibliographical references and index.
Audience: Grades 5-8.
ISBN 978-1-4777-7563-9 (library bound)—ISBN 978-1-4777-7565-3 (pbk.)—ISBN 978-1-4777-7566-0 (6-pack)
1. Mass media and technology—Juvenile literature. 2. Multimedia systems—Evaluation—Juvenile literature. 3. Communication—Technological innovations—Juvenile literature. 4. Human-computer interaction—Juvenile literature. 5. Readers (Middle school) I. Parente, Robin W. II. Title. III. Title: Tips and tricks for evaluating multimedia content.
P96.T42A87 2015
372.47'2—dc23

2014010040

Manufactured in the United States of America

Contents

Introduction

The Common Core Reading Standards are a set of skills designed to prepare you for entering college or beginning your career. They're grouped into broad College and Career Readiness Anchor Standards, and they help you use reasoning and evidence in ways that will serve you well now and in the future.

The skills build from kindergarten to the twelfth grade. Grades six through eight take the spotlight here. You may already have noticed changes in your classrooms that are based on the standards—deeper-level reading, shorter passages, an emphasis on informational texts, or an overall increase in rigor within your daily activities.

This book will help you understand, practice, and independently apply the skills through easy-to-use tips and tricks. Gaining mastery of the skills is the goal.

The reading standards for evaluating multimedia content incorporate writing, speaking, and listening standards that are relevant for gathering, assessing, and applying information.

Your teachers may use close reading for some of their instruction. During close reading, you read shorter passages more deeply and analytically. Close reading passages often have rich, complex content. They contain grade-level vocabulary words, sentence structures, and literary techniques. Reading a short three-page passage closely could take two to three days or more. The benefit to you is that you get a deeper, more valuable understanding of what you've read. Close reading is a critical part of the new Common Core Reading Standards and is an approach used with literature (fiction) and informational text (nonfiction).

The focus of this book, however, is not on reading the main passage of a text closely. Instead, it is on exploring the other types of diverse media that are often used to support a main passage. In essence, we will use a "close reading" approach to explore multimedia content.

This book focuses on Anchor Standard 7: Integrate and evaluate content presented in diverse formats and media, including visually and quantitatively, as well as in words. In the next chapter, we'll break this standard apart and look at it closely. Also, the tips and tricks that can help you gain mastery of this standard are introduced.

In the passages that follow, you tag along with expert readers. These skilled experts share their brief summary of the main passage (remember that they've already spent considerable time close reading the main passage, which is reproduced here as "Source 1" for your use and reference, when appropriate). Next, they think aloud while "close reading" multimedia content that has been paired with the main passages. Visual icons that represent the tips and tricks appear in the margins and prompt the expert reader. Ways in which the expert reader applies them appear in "expert reader" margin notes. You'll also observe how the expert readers organize their thoughts and evaluate the media in graphic organizers, respond to multiple short-answer questions, and reflect on the ways in which their learning has been enriched through their experience with the multimedia content.

After you gain an understanding of how the skills are applied, it's your turn to try with guided practice. You'll apply the skills independently and perform a self-evaluation by checking your responses against the answers provided. Based on your responses, you can determine if another pass through the expert reader's examples might be helpful—or if you've mastered the skill.

CHAPTER 1

A QUICK AND EASY OVERVIEW: THE SKILLS AND THE TIPS & TRICKS

Let's examine the skills of integrating and evaluating multimedia content so that we understand them. First, it's important to understand that the term "multimedia content" means materials presented through different media or formats, such as audio, video, film, stage performances, photographs, interactive media, charts or graphics, and others. As mentioned earlier, the emphasis of this standard is on extending your literacy skills beyond reading the printed words in a text passage. Exploring other media versions of a literary work or investigating the types of diverse media that often accompany informational text can enrich your appreciation or understanding of an idea, event, or topic.

The word "integrate" means to join together with or combine. It's no surprise that one way to work with multimedia content is to consider ways in which you can join together or combine the knowledge you gain from varied media sources. Not only can you deepen your understanding of a topic or idea through a multimedia experience, you can broaden your knowledge, too.

This standard focuses on building skills to evaluate multimedia content, such as stage performances, audio, video, film, photographs, interactive media, charts or graphics, and more.

The word "evaluate" means to weigh the advantages and disadvantages of a particular media approach. Another way to evaluate could be looking at the similarities and differences between or among multiple media formats. Determining the unique features of the various media and exploring how those features may affect your experience is explored here.

These skills are useful as you read literature and informational text, and in reading within history/social studies, science, and technical subjects. Also, as you progress in grade levels, the depth and scope of your evaluation of multimedia content should increase.

Tips & Tricks

There are several easy-to-use tips and tricks that can help you evaluate multimedia content. As you'll see, many are organized by media type and are referred to as "checklists." However, it's important to remember to use the tips and tricks flexibly. Media content can vary greatly, and your evaluation could be strengthened by reviewing features that are listed in multiple media categories. As you gain experience, your ability to wield these strategies effectively will sharpen.

The icons featured below are used in subsequent chapters to show you how the tips and tricks are used in action with literature and informational texts. As you shall see, some strategies are more suited to a particular genre.

Launching "Jump-Start" Clues: Before you begin your evaluation, you may wish to first identify the type of media you will be exploring and how you will experience its message. Identifying the media and then reflecting on the ways in which you will construct its meaning can ignite your senses into action—you'll know what to look for, what to listen to, or what to *take in* through multiple senses from the start.

Audio Recordings Checklist: Audio recordings are sometimes referred to as "readings" and may be used to supplement written literature, such as poetry and stories. They may also feature speeches or other kinds of important informational content that is delivered or presented to an audience. There are many things to listen for in an audio recording. Notice if the speaker stresses words or phrases by adjusting volume, pitch, or tone. Also pay attention to the rhythm and detect pauses, repetition, and other ways in which the speaker controls the pacing of the delivery. Can you sense a mood? Are there other features added to the words, such as music, audience responses, or speaker interjections or comments? An emotional message can be conveyed through the manner in which a reader expresses words and ideas in an audio recording.

 ●**Images, Photographs, and Artwork Checklist:** These can include cartoons, photographs, posters, and other types of image-based artwork used to supplement informational text or illustrate ideas in some genres of literature. Through their use, viewers are able to grasp a wealth of ideas quickly.

Cartoons convey a message through humor yet must be viewed in the context of the time in which they were created. Additionally, it's important to notice the content and think about why the artist featured characters or events in a certain way.

There are many features to notice in photographs, posters, and artwork as well. Pay attention to the details that comprise the content, the angle or vantage point from which the photo was taken, the use of color or the absence of it, and the tone or mood of the photograph. Notice if something stands out and draws your attention.

Other types of visuals could include illustrations that reinforce or extend ideas in a text. It's important to consider ways in which the artwork contributes to your understanding and to describe how it achieves this. Does the artwork clarify a difficult concept? Does it feature a critical event from a story? In what ways is the artwork useful?

 ●**Maps, Diagrams, Charts, and Interactive Media Checklist:** Maps are used to depict ideas within a geographic or location-based context. They are often used to reinforce ideas expressed in informational text and in some genres of literature. They may cover vast or very narrow areas and may include guides, such as a legend or key. There are many features to notice on a map, such as the content or area featured, the scale, the use of color or pattern to convey a message, and more. It's also important to notice the ways in which an author interjects ideas in a map. Notice if your attention is drawn to a particular area.

The same considerations should be given to charts and interactive media. Determine the content, the manner in which the content is conveyed, and what message authors share through their choices. Decisions about what information will be conveyed and how it will be conveyed are intentional. Determining the reasons for these decisions can help you interpret the content. Interactive media requires viewers to take an active role in order to interpret information. This, too, becomes a key matter to evaluate with this type of media.

● **Video Renditions and Live Performances Checklist:** A video rendition could include a movie version of a work of literature. Here, the rendition is used to tell a story that first appeared in text format. Some degree of creative liberty is often taken by a director or filmmaker to make use of different technology, in consideration of an audience, or for other reasons. The same type of considerations can apply to live performances. Here, producers consider ways in which the actors, staging, props, and other theatrical elements can interact to present ideas that appear in texts. Some changes or adaptations may be made. For these types of media, it's important to consider ways in which the video or performance stays faithful to or departs from the original. Analyzing all elements, including depictions of the setting, characters, events, conflicts/resolutions, and the theme, should be carefully evaluated.

Video renditions can also be informational in content. Interviews with experts, historians, and people who were involved in the events being featured may be included. Video footage is usually used to complement audio information. This footage may help a viewer begin to more clearly understand an event or time period that he or she is unfamiliar with. Similar to authors of informational text, videographers have information they want the viewer to know. The viewer needs to listen and watch carefully to determine what is most important and take what is needed to enhance his or her understanding, since these video renditions frequently have a large amount of information presented within a short period of time.

● **Tune in to Your Inner Voice:** Keep in mind that the media checklists include some things to look and listen for. You might uncover others as your mind actively constructs meaning from the content of what you take in during your multimedia experience. Monitoring your thoughts is critical. It's also important to remember that you are viewing the media with background knowledge that you've gained from your previous reading. This should affect your views.

● **Avoid Common Pitfalls:** Sometimes we can become distracted by something in the media, which could steer us away from an artist's, producer's, or reader's intended meaning. Staying engaged and focused while ensuring that your ideas square with evidence is critical. Also keep in mind that your school library media specialist is an excellent resource to help you with most matters relating to multimedia content.

CHAPTER 2

EVALUATING MULTIMEDIA CONTENT AND LITERATURE: EXPERT READER MODEL

Let's see how to apply the tips and tricks of evaluating multimedia content to literature. Remember, literature could be adventure stories, historical fiction, mysteries, myths, science fiction, realistic fiction, poems, fantasy, and more.

Plan of Action

In this chapter, you will explore two distinct multimedia experiences. The first centers on poetry, and the second, a work of fiction. As discussed earlier, when applying this standard to works of literature, you would most likely begin by reading the main passage in its written version. Typically, you would use a close reading approach and apply other Common Core skills you would be learning in your classroom. Here, we are modifying that process by providing expert reader summaries of their close reading experience. Let's begin with the multimedia poetry experience.

Walt Whitman (1819—1892) is considered one of America's most influential poets of the nineteenth century.

Multimedia Experience with Poetry

Source 1 is the printed version of the poem "O Captain! My Captain!" by Walt Whitman. Source 2 is an audio recording of the poem. Here, only one printed version of the poem has been reproduced. Please follow these directions: (1) read the printed version without referring to the expert reader margin notes, (2) read the expert reader's close reading summary, and (3) refer to the audio access (Source 2) directions, featured below.

Source 1: Printed Text Version
Source 2: Audio Recording by Tracy Hall

📖 EXPERT READER:

🏃 I know I will be listening to an audio reading of this Walt Whitman poem. Based on the expert reader's summary, I know this is a poem about Abraham Lincoln's death. I suspect the reading will be emotional beginning with the title, which features exclamation points. I'm prepared to listen carefully for stressed words, pacing, and other features often found in poetry readings.

🔊 The reader emphasizes the words "O Captain" with excitement and continues the line as if sharing a successful event with a good friend. I hear how the reader has interpreted the poet's use of the apostrophe poetic technique.

🔊 The reader pauses, and I hear a change in the tone of her voice. With each successive use of the word "heart," I can sense in the reader's voice that there is something painfully wrong.

🔊 The rhyme scheme in this stanza is accentuated by the reader's powerful articulation. I hear the harshness of the words "red" and "dead."

🔊 The first four lines in this stanza sound cheerful throughout the gentle prodding to get the Captain to arise. The exalted excitement that I heard in the reader's voice during her reading of the first four lines in the first stanza is resumed. In this audio version of the poem, I can hear how Whitman both celebrates Lincoln's accomplishments and mourns his death.

💬 In the last four lines of this stanza, the reader pauses, expressing astonishment as if a "dream" that the Captain will not arise. I can hear the anguish and disbelief.

🔊 The somber tone of the first four lines of this stanza suggests that there is now no doubt, no disbelief—the Captain is dead.

🔊 The reader slows the pacing of the last four lines and stresses the word "I," which helps me recognize the poet's personal feelings of loss. The reader also pauses in the last line, which heightens the emotional impact of the poem.

"O Captain! My Captain!"
by Walt Whitman 🏃

O CAPTAIN! my Captain! our fearful trip is done; 🔊
The ship has weather'd every rack, the prize we sought is won;
The port is near, the bells I hear, the people all exulting,
While follow eyes the steady keel, the vessel grim and daring:
  But O heart! heart! heart! 🔊
   O the bleeding drops of red,
    Where on the deck my Captain lies,
    Fallen cold and dead. 🔊

O Captain! my Captain! rise up and hear the bells;
Rise up—for you the flag is flung—for you the bugle trills;
For you bouquets and ribbon'd wreaths—for you the shores a-crowding;
For you they call, the swaying mass, their eager faces turning; 🔊
  Here Captain! dear father!
   This arm beneath your head;
    It is some dream that on the deck, 💬
    You've fallen cold and dead.

My Captain does not answer, his lips are pale and still;
My father does not feel my arm, he has no pulse nor will; 🔊
The ship is anchor'd safe and sound, its voyage closed and done;
From fearful trip, the victor ship, comes in with object won;
  Exult, O shores, and ring, O bells!
   But I, with mournful tread, 🔊
    Walk the deck my Captain lies,
    Fallen cold and dead.

Expert Reader's Close Reading Summary

Walt Whitman has written this poem to both mourn the assassination death of Abraham Lincoln and to celebrate his very critical accomplishments. The "ship" represents the journey of the United States through the weathering times of the Civil War. The "Captain" represents Abraham Lincoln, a leader the crowds admire and honor with bells, ribbons, flag waving, and more. Through the use of this extended metaphor, Whitman dramatically captures the turbulence that challenged the nation and Lincoln's successful navigation through it. Yet the tragedy and astonishment of Lincoln's death is emphasized and lingers.

Audio Access Directions

Now that we have some background information, let's listen to an audio recording of the poem. To access the recording, Source 2, go to https://librivox.org/o-captain-my-captain-by-walt-whitman and then scroll down and select "Version 13" read by Tracy Hall. A good strategy for listening to this short audio reading is to listen to it in its entirety to get the gist. Then listen to it again (and possibly a third time) and follow along with the printed version above, this time reading the expert reader notes to see how she demonstrates use of the tips and tricks to capture important information that helps build knowledge.

Now let's see how the expert reader compares and contrasts the experience of reading and listening to the poem. Following this comparison, the expert reader shares her reflection on her multimedia poetry experience.

Listening	Shared	Reading
The reader's expression and pacing help me interpret the changing emotional tone of the poem.		By focusing on the "look" of the poem, I can appreciate the poem's structure.
As the reader stresses certain words, this helps me gain new insights about ideas that the poet emphasizes.	Both versions contain the same content, which allows me to evaluate the methods of delivery.	The use of punctuation cues me into the poet's meaning and intentions. I also see special treatment of words like "weather'd," "ribbon'd," and "anchor'd."
I can hear the power of the end rhyme, and I better grasp that some words and ideas are more important than others based on the reader's articulation.		In the printed version, I can see that the poet uses end rhyme. In some cases, I can also see that he uses repetition.

Expert Reader Reflection

The audio version helps me better hear and understand the poet's use of some technique, like rhyme and meter. This, in turn, enables me to better understand the emotional meaning of the words and ideas. Now I can understand how a multimedia experience can deepen my knowledge.

Let's see how the expert reader tackles a short answer question that show her skill at evaluating Source 2 and integrating her new knowledge into her overall understanding of the poem.

Question: How does the audio version reinforce the meaning of the poem?

Expert Reader: Through the use of tone, pacing, articulation, and expression, the speaker is able to add emotional impact to the printed words. From the audio reading, we experience joy over the great successes of the "trip" and the adoration of the crowds for their "Captain." Likewise, through the same audio techniques, we experience a deep loss and mourning over the "Captain's" death. These emotional ups and downs, which are evident in the audio version, capture the dual meaning of the poem—to mourn the death of Lincoln while also celebrating his great accomplishments. The audio version reinforces these ideas in a way that is not as evident in the printed version.

Multimedia Experience with Fiction

Now let's move to another type of multimedia experience involving the literary classic *The Wonderful Wizard of Oz* by L. Frank Baum. Source 1 is a printed excerpt from the book, and you will also evaluate a clip from a video production version, identified as Source 2. Like before, only one printed version of the original text has been reproduced. Please follow these directions: (1) read the printed version without referring to the expert reader margin notes, (2) read the expert reader's close reading summary, and (3) refer to the video access (Source 2) directions, featured below.

Source 1: Printed Text Version (Excerpts from Chapters 1 and 2)
Source 2: Video Rendition

The Wonderful Wizard of Oz
by L. Frank Baum

Dorothy lived in the midst of the great Kansas prairies, with Uncle Henry, who was a farmer, and Aunt Em, who was the farmer's wife. Their house was small and had once been painted, but the sun blistered the paint and the rains washed it away. Now it was as dull and gray as everything else.

EXPERT READER:

I know I will be viewing a video clip from this classic work. The expert reader summary provided me with a good summary of the significant elements that are featured in this part clip carefully, watching for ways in which it departs and remains true to the original text.

I notice how the producer reflects the drab Kansas prairie setting through the use of black and white film. Here, he has used a film technique that enhances the meaning of the text.

The Wonderful Wizard of Oz by L. Frank Baum is another work of literature explored through multimedia in this chapter.

It was Toto that made Dorothy laugh, and saved her from growing as gray as her other surroundings. Today, however, they were not playing. Uncle Henry sat upon the doorstep and looked anxiously at the sky, which was even grayer than usual. Suddenly he stood up.

"There's a cyclone coming, Em," he called. "I'll go look after the stock."

Aunt Em dropped her work and came to the door. "Quick, Dorothy!" she screamed. "Run for the cellar!"

Toto jumped out of Dorothy's arms and hid under the bed, and the girl started to get him. Aunt Em, badly frightened, threw open the trap door in the floor and climbed down the ladder into the cellar. Dorothy caught Toto at last and started to follow her aunt. When she was halfway across the room there came a great shriek from the wind, and the house shook so hard that she lost her footing and sat down suddenly upon the floor. Then a strange thing happened.

The house whirled around and rose slowly through the air, higher and higher, until it was at the very top of the cyclone; and there it remained and was carried for miles. It was dark, and the wind howled horribly around her. Yet as hours passed, Dorothy slowly got over her fright and at last crawled over the swaying floor to her bed, where she lay down and soon closed her eyes and fell fast asleep.

EXPERT READER:

The movie clip strays from the text; in the clip Dorothy is with Professor Marvel when the storm arrives, while in the text she is at home.

I'm beginning to see that the action in the movie departs pretty dramatically from the text. For example, in the film clip, Dorothy is saying good-bye to Professor Marvel (a character not mentioned in the text) and is returning home when the storm hits. Still, the main theme of a bad storm launching an unexpected adventure remains unaltered. I'll monitor this.

Events in the film clip include much more drama. Specifically, Aunt Em calls for Dorothy amidst howling winds and a swirling funnel cloud. Uncle Henry calls everyone to the storm cellar. There is panic over Dorothy's absence. Dorothy returns to the farm yet is unable to open the cellar door. She is hit by a window in the house, falls on her bed, and dozes off, as a collage of scenes—from farm events to witches—floats by the open window to music.

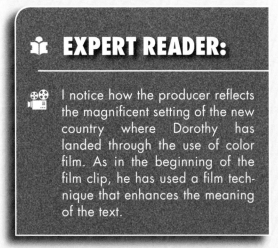

EXPERT READER:

I notice how the producer reflects the magnificent setting of the new country where Dorothy has landed through the use of color film. As in the beginning of the film clip, he has used a film technique that enhances the meaning of the text.

Awakened by a sudden shock, she sprang from her bed and ran and opened the door. The little girl gave a cry of amazement and looked about her, her eyes growing bigger at the wonderful sights she saw. The cyclone had set the house down gently in a country of marvelous beauty. There were lovely patches of greensward all about, with stately trees bearing rich and luscious fruits. Banks of gorgeous flowers were on every hand, and birds with rare and brilliant plumage sang and fluttered in the trees and bushes.

Expert Reader's Close Reading Summary: In these two chapters, Baum introduces the characters, establishes two very different kinds of settings (the drab Kansas prairie and the country of marvelous beauty), and launches the problem in the story: Dorothy and Toto have been swept away in a cyclone. Although the events in these chapters are highly unlikely, Baum permits us to suspend our disbelief through his use of a third-person narrator, who remarks as the house begins to swirl within the cyclone: "Then a strange thing happened." We recognize that things aren't quite believable, yet are more eager to learn about this new land and the likely adventures that will unfold.

Video Access Directions

Now let's access a video rendering of the scenes depicted in the text, which we'll call Source 2. Go to http://www.dailymotion.com and search and select "The Wonderful Wizard of Oz - Judy Garland – The

Cyclone Scene" (04:46). A good strategy for using short video clips is to first view the clip in its entirety to get the gist. Then view it a second (and perhaps a third) time and follow along with the printed version above, this time reading the expert reader's notes to see how he demonstrates the use of the tips and tricks to evaluate this content through the use of comparing and contrasting. You may wish to use the pause function as needed.

Now let's see how the expert reader uses this diagram graphic organizer to compare ways in which the video performance stays faithful and where it departs from the original.

Video Rendition (Listening and Viewing)	Shared	Text Version (Reading)
The movie clip introduces other characters, some through special techniques.	The Kansas farm is a drab setting.	Three main characters are introduced.
Dorothy is away from the farm yet returns home as the cyclone arrives.	A cyclone strikes, Dorothy is swept into the storm, and she lands safely in a new place.	Dorothy remains at the farm as the cyclone arrives.
Dramatic sight and sound scenes depict the cyclone, chaos on the farm, Dorothy's ride through the storm, and the vibrant landing through multiple angles.	The new area where Dorothy lands is colorful and vibrant.	A narrator briefly describes the cyclone, explains the house getting swept away as a "strange" happening, and describes the new land.

Expert Reader Reflection

The video rendition helps me see and hear the cyclone. I'm frightened by its force, and I feel badly for Dorothy and her misfortune. The video rendition draws me into the story much more deeply. It also makes me believe in the impossible and makes me eager to follow Dorothy's adventure.

Let's see how the expert reader tackles a short-answer question that shows his skill at evaluating Source 2.

Question: Does the video clip rendition stay faithful to the original text?

The video clip rendition is faithful to the original text. Although there are some differences between the two versions, the director uses special video techniques that enhance events without altering the main intent of the author, L. Frank Baum. For example, the director uses black-and-white tones for the Kansas setting and then color tones for the setting of the new area where Dorothy lands. Even though the director introduces new characters, deviates somewhat from the story-line, and dramatizes events such as the swirling cyclone, the main idea that Dorothy is transported to an unusual place far away remains intact.

Conclusion

How well do you feel you've grasped the expert reader's use of tips and tricks for evaluating multimedia content? Decide if you're ready to move on to the guided practice in the next chapter or if you would like to take another pass through the expert reader's model.

CHAPTER 3

EVALUATING MULTIMEDIA CONTENT AND LITERATURE: GUIDED PRACTICE

Now it's time for you to practice applying the tips and tricks as you compare and contrast multimedia experiences for works of literature. As in the earlier chapter, you will explore two distinct multimedia experiences. The first centers on poetry, and the second, a work of fiction. As discussed earlier, when applying this standard to works of literature, you would most likely begin by reading the main passage in its written version. Typically, you would use a close reading approach and apply other Common Core skills you would be learning in your classroom. Here, we are modifying that process by providing expert reader summaries of their close reading experience. Let's begin with the multimedia poetry experience.

Multimedia Experience with Poetry

Source 1 is the printed version of the poem "I Wandered Lonely as a Cloud (Daffodils)" by William Wordsworth. Source 2 is an audio recording of the poem. Here, only one printed version of the poem has been reproduced. Please follow these directions: (1) read the printed version without referring to the guided practice margin notes, (2) read

WORDSWORTH.

Bowness. July 18th 1904.

William Wordsworth (1770—1850) was a British writer who gained acclaim for his lyrical ballads. The poem featured in this chapter is believed to be based on an experience the poet shared with his sister when the pair unexpectedly came across a field of daffodils.

the expert reader's close reading summary, and (3) refer to the audio access (Source 2) directions, featured below.

Source 1: Printed Text Version

Source 2: Audio Recording by Graham Williams

GUIDED PRACTICE PROMPT:

What do you know about audio recordings to support and build understanding? Possible response: I know an audio recording can help me interpret the meaning of a poem. The reader may stress words, alter the rhythm, and/or create mood through the delivery. An emotional message can be conveyed through the use of these techniques.

"I Wandered Lonely as a Cloud (Daffodils)"
by William Wordsworth

I wandered lonely as a Cloud
That floats on high o'er vales and Hills,
When all at once I saw a crowd,
A host, of golden Daffodils;
Beside the Lake, beneath the trees,

Fluttering and dancing in the breeze.
Continuous as the stars that shine
And twinkle on the milky way,
They stretched in never-ending line
Along the margin of a bay:
Ten thousand saw I at a glance,
Tossing their heads in sprightly dance. (MP3)

The waves beside them danced; but they
Out-did the sparkling waves in glee:
A Poet could not but be gay,
In such a jocund company:
I gazed—and gazed—but little thought
What wealth the show to me had brought:

For oft, when on my couch I lie
In vacant or in pensive mood,
They flash upon that inward eye
Which is the bliss of solitude;
And then my heart with pleasure fills,
And dances with the Daffodils. (MP3)

Expert Reader Summary: This simple yet uplifting poem recounts a speaker's experience overcoming feelings of loneliness. While passing a lake, he notices vast fields of daffodils that looked as if they were dancing in the breeze. This vision of beauty and joy replaced the speaker's feeling of loneliness. Still, he did not fully recognize the value of the scene until he later realized that he could recall it at will to help cheer him up when needed.

GUIDED PRACTICE PROMPT:

(MP3) In what way has the audio recording helped you interpret the poem? Possible response: In this stanza, I hear the reader stress the word "host" to support the vast quantity of daffodils the speaker spies. I also hear the reader's tone lighten over the course of the last three lines of the stanza as if to reflect the speaker's changing mood. Finally, the use of the simile in the first line and personification in the last line come to life through the reader's delivery.

(MP3) Does the audio recording help you hear some of the poetic technique used in the poem? Possible response: I can hear the repeating ABABCC rhyme pattern that adds to the cheerfulness of the tone and the fluid rhythm of the poem. Also in this stanza, the reader brings to life the use of simile and personification.

What are you thinking? Possible response: I hear the unusual construction of some of the lines of the poems, which could be the technique of poetic inversion. For example in this stanza, the line "A poet could not but be gay" lingers because of the unusual sound of the order of words. Perhaps this is done for rhyming purposes.

(MP3) In what way has the audio recording helped you interpret the poem? Possible response: In the final stanza I can hear the reader stress the word "pleasure." I also notice that he alters his pacing and slows down while reading the last line of the poem. This is a thoughtful way to end a poem as if a slow, finale to a dance.

Audio Access Directions

Now that we have some background information, let's listen to an audio recording of the poem. To access the recording, Source 2, go to https://librivox.org/i-wandered-lonely-as-a-cloud-by-william-wordsworth and then scroll down and select "Version 04" read by Graham Williams. A good strategy for listening to this short audio reading is to listen to it in its entirety to get the gist. Then listen to it again (and possibly a third time) and follow along with the printed version above, this time reading the guided practice prompts, responding to the prompts, and checking your responses against those provided.

Now try to complete a graphic organizer that compares and contrasts your experience of reading and listening to the different versions of the poem. See if your answers agree with some of the possible responses provided below. Then try to jot down a brief reflection on your multimedia poetry experience. Again, you can refer to the possible response as needed.

Possible Response for Graphic Organizer:

Listening	Shared	Reading
The reader's expression and pacing help me sense the changing mood in the poem.		By focusing on the "look" of the poem, I can appreciate the poem's tight structure.
The reader stresses words that help suggest areas of emphasis. I also appreciate visual images that are triggered through the reader's delivery of the similes and metaphors.	Both versions contain the same content, which allows me to evaluate the methods of delivery.	The use of punctuation cues me into the poet's meaning and intentions. I can also see that the poet uses multiple poetic techniques.
I can hear the power of the rhyme and inversion and appreciate the simple, lyrical sound of the poem as a whole.		I can see that some of the lines contain unusual construction.

Expert Reader Reflection

The audio version helps me better hear and "see" the poet's use of some techniques, including rhyme, inversion, metaphor, and simile. This, in turn, enables me to take in a fuller, richer experience from the poem. The multimedia experience deepens the impact of my experience with the poem.

Now try a short-answer response. Talk your answer through or jot it down on a separate piece of paper. Then check your response against the possible response provided.

Question: How does the audio version reinforce the meaning of the poem?

Possible Response: Through the use of many techniques that enhance the sound and the sights of the poem, I can appreciate how a recollection of a vast field of daffodils could become a gift that could alter someone's mood. In the audio version of the poem, you can detect the speaker's mood change. Likewise, the lyrical delivery helps trigger the visual images that allow me to further engage deeply with the poem.

Multimedia Experience with Fiction

Now let's move to another type of multimedia experience. Like the expert reader, you will be working with the literary classic *The Wonderful Wizard of Oz* by L. Frank Baum. Source 1 is a printed excerpt from the book, and you will also evaluate a clip from a video production version, identified as Source 2. Like before, only one printed version of the original text has been reproduced. Please follow these directions: (1) read the printed version without referring to the guided practice margin notes, (2) read the expert reader's close reading summary, and (3) refer to the video access (Source 2) directions, featured below.

Source 1: Printed Text Version (Excerpt from Chapter 3: How Dorothy Saved the Scarecrow)

Source 2: Video Rendition

🖥 GUIDED PRACTICE PROMPT:

🏃 What do you know about video renditions that may affect your evaluation of this media content? Possible response: I know that I should look for ways in which the content is different from and similar to the content of book. My evaluation should address this type of comparison.

🎥 Do you notice where and why the producer may have veered from the text version? I notice how the producer has mostly remained true to the story. The plot is intact, as Dorothy helps the Scarecrow down from the pole where he hangs. However, the producer uses a song in the video to inform the audience of the Scarecrow's lack of brains, which is very engaging.

The Wonderful Wizard of Oz
by L. Frank Baum 🏃

Dressed in her blue and white checked gingham dress and silver shoes that had belonged to the Witch of the East, Dorothy set off for Emerald City to ask the Great Oz for help returning to Kansas. Soon she came upon a scarecrow placed high on a pole and was surprised when he spoke. He complained of being stuck on his pole, so Dorothy removed him. After learning of Dorothy's purpose for heading to Emerald City, the Scarecrow reveals he has no brains.

"Do you think," he asked, "if I go to the Emerald City with you, that Oz would give me some brains?"

"I cannot tell," she returned, "but you may come with me, if you like. If Oz will not give you any brains you will be no worse off than you are now." 🎥

"That is true," said the Scarecrow. "You see," he continued confidentially, "I don't mind my legs and arms and body being stuffed, because I cannot get hurt. If anyone treads on my toes or sticks a pin into me, it doesn't matter, for I can't feel it. But I do not want people to call me a fool, and if my head stays stuffed with straw instead of with brains, how am I ever to know anything?

"I understand how you feel," said the little girl, who was truly sorry for him. "If you will come with me I'll ask Oz to do all he can for you."

"Thank you," he answered gratefully.

They started along the path of yellow brick for the Emerald City.

Toto did not like this addition to the party at first, and he often growled in an unfriendly way at the Scarecrow.

"Don't mind Toto," said Dorothy to her new friend. "He never bites."

"Oh, I'm not afraid," replied the Scarecrow. "He can't hurt the straw. There is only one thing in the world I am afraid of."

"What is that?" asked Dorothy.

"It's a lighted match," answered the Scarecrow.

GUIDED PRACTICE PROMPT:

Do you notice how the producer makes use of the actors' talents in the video? Possible response: The dialogue between Dorothy and the Scarecrow also remains mostly aligned to the original text. Yet the Scarecrow's plight is depicted in a less severe manner. Through song and dance, the Scarecrow shares the kind of lighthearted gains he seeks. The producer uses the talents of the actor in a way that is unique to this media, and we immediately hope for his success.

What are you thinking about the mood of the story? Possible response: As the pair begins their journey, they are cheerful and excited. Through the many sights and sounds we take in, we sense their enthusiasm, which is largely absent from the text version.

Why might both versions include dialogue that captures the Scarecrow's fears? Possible response: It's possible that both the author and the producer wanted to use foreshadowing as a way of creating some tension as the plot unfolds.

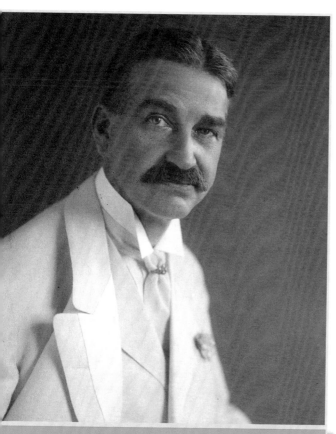

Lyman Frank Baum (1856—1919) was an American author of children's books. Better known as L. Frank Baum, he is remembered most as the author of the well-loved classic *The Wonderful Wizard of Oz*.

Expert Reader's Close Reading Summary

In this chapter, Baum introduces the Scarecrow character and reveals the reason why he would be a good companion to venture to Emerald City with Dorothy— he hopes to ask the Wizard for a brain. Dorothy is not the only character with a problem to overcome. With the addition of the Scarecrow, the story expands and becomes more interesting and engaging. We also suspect that the Scarecrow's fear—a lighted match—could foreshadow events that are likely to happen as the pair's adventure to the Emerald City takes shape. This uneasiness is sure to keep us turning pages.

Video Access Directions

Now let's access a video rendering of the scenes depicted in the text, which we'll call Source 2. Go to www.dailymotion.com and search and select "The Wonderful Wizard of Oz/xmj210_the-scarecrow-joins-doro- thy-from-the-wizard-of-os-1" (01:33). A good strategy for using short video clips is to first view the clip in its entirety to get the gist. Then view it a second (and perhaps a third) time and follow along with the printed version above, this time reading the guided prompts, responding to the prompts, and checking your responses against those provided. You may wish to use the pause function as needed.

Now try to complete a graphic organizer that compares and contrasts your experience of reading and listening to the different versions of the text. You can check your answers against suggestions provided below. Then write a reflection on your multimedia experience with fiction. Again you can refer to the possible response provided.

Possible Response for Graphic Organizer:

Video Rendition (Listening and Viewing)	Shared	Text Version (Reading)
The movie clip introduces the Scarecrow as a highly likeable character despite his many struggles.	The Scarecrow is propped uncomfortably on a pole, and he laments his misfortune of not having a brain.	The Scarecrow is a mildly flat character.
The Scarecrow shares the kind of positive yet whimsical changes he expects should he receive a brain.	The Scarecrow asks Dorothy if he can accompany her to visit the Wizard, where he will ask for a brain.	The Scarecrow's reason for wanting a brain is that he does not want to be considered a fool.
Dramatic scenes depict the Scarecrow and Dorothy singing, dancing, and frolicking down the yellow brick road.	The Scarecrow reveals his one fear—a lighted match.	Events unfold largely through character dialogue

Possible Reader Reflection

Through numerous techniques, the video rendition helps bring to life the charming character of the Scarecrow. He has a large personality, we instantly like him, and we want him to overcome his challenges and be successful. The video rendition draws me into the story much more deeply. I am emotionally invested in the Scarecrow's success. I am eager to follow the pair's adventures.

Now try a short answer response that helps you evaluate Source 2. Talk your answer through or jot it down on a separate piece of paper. Then check your response against the possible response provided.

Question: Does the video clip rendition stay faithful to the original text?

Possible Response: For the most part, this video rendition remains faithful to the original text. In the video, Dorothy looks as she is described in the text, and her encounter with the Scarecrow contains the events that are presented in the text. However, the video version differs greatly by including both song and dance that are not included in the book. Clearly, the producer takes creative liberty to enhance a viewer's experience by incorporating techniques that are unique to the video media.

Conclusion

How well do you feel you've grasped the use of tips and tricks for evaluating multimedia content and literature? Were your answers similar to those provided by the expert reader? Decide if you're ready to move on to the next chapter, where you will explore multimedia experiences and informational text, or if you would like to take another pass through these examples.

CHAPTER 4

EVALUATING MULTIMEDIA CONTENT AND INFORMATIONAL TEXT: EXPERT READER MODEL

Now let's see how to apply the tips and tricks to informational text. Informational text is a type of nonfiction, or factual text, that is written to inform the reader, explain something, or convey information about the natural and social worlds. Informational text can include newspaper articles; magazine articles; autobiographies; historical, scientific, technical, or economic accounts; and more.

When you begin exploring a new topic that you may have limited experience with, it can be helpful to integrate written text with information from multimedia sources to expand your knowledge and fill in any gaps in your understanding. Each multimedia content area has its own unique advantages and may help you create a solid foundation of understanding.

Plan of Action

In this chapter, you will be integrating written text with multimedia to learn about the Great Chicago Fire of 1871. In addition to the written text, you will be examining and evaluating a short video, several

THE GREAT FIRE AT CHICAGO OCT.9ᵀᴴ 1871. VIEW FROM THE WEST SIDE.

Nearly eighteen thousand buildings were destroyed in the Chicago Fire of 1871.

pieces of artwork that were made during the time period, and several maps to build and strengthen your knowledge of this disaster.

As mentioned in chapter 2, when applying this standard to informational text, you would most likely begin by reading a passage. A close reading approach would be used while applying other Common Core skills being practiced in your classroom. The written passage features an expert reader's summary, which will help you comprehend the passage in a way that would closely duplicate your own close reading of it. You will want to read the passage and summary carefully before accessing the multimedia content. You will then access the multimedia material and tag along as the expert reader applies the tips and tricks and creates graphic organizers to build knowledge on this topic. Finally, you'll see how the expert reader answers short response questions that demonstrate how to evaluate multimedia content and informational text.

Following these activities, it will be your turn to practice. In chapter 5, you'll be evaluating multimedia content using practice prompts. You can check your thinking against responses provided.

Source 1

An Excerpt from
The Great Chicago Fire of 1871
by Christy Marx

On the evening of October 8, 1871, more than 300,000 weary residents of the great city of Chicago went to bed expecting nothing more than a quiet night's sleep followed by an ordinary Monday. Instead, these unprepared citizens found themselves pursued by an inferno, driven into the waters of Lake Michigan or running far onto the open prairie north and west of the city. The people of Chicago were chased out of their city by one of the most destructive fires the world had ever seen.

The walls of flames roared and rumbled with a terrifying noise. Burning debris rose into the air on hurricane-like winds. The fire raced with such speed that it literally nipped at the heels of those who ran from it. The inferno destroyed entire buildings in minutes.

From the night of October 8 to the early morning of October 10, the Great Chicago Fire burned away nearly the entire city, destroying 18,000 buildings, from the humble shacks of the poor to the finest brick and marble homes of the rich. The fire leveled banks, stores, government buildings, restaurants, schools, and churches—nothing could stand in its way. Enormous lumber mills, warehouses, and factories of all kinds were burned to the ground. Priceless works of art, museums, and libraries were devoured. Countless numbers of pets and livestock were lost.

Amazingly, less than 300 people were killed in the fire. But afterward, more than 90,000 people were left without shelter, food, water, or anything more than the clothes they were wearing or the few precious possessions they managed to carry with them at the last minute.

People looked for someone—or something—to blame: foreign anarchists trying to overthrow the government, irresponsible firefighters who had been drinking, and most famous, Mrs. O'Leary's cow who knocked over an oil lantern, setting the barn ablaze. None of these are true. The sad fact is Chicago was a city that was just waiting to burn down.

Expert Reader's Close Reading Summary

In October of 1871, one of the most destructive fires the world has ever seen raced through Chicago. People were driven from their homes by a raging inferno and escaped to safety with little else than the clothing they were wearing and whatever they could carry. The fire destroyed all the buildings in its path and left ninety thousand people homeless. Less than three hundred people were killed, but nearly everything in the city of Chicago was destroyed by the fire. Although there were many theories for the cause of the fire, the author states that Chicago was a city "just waiting to burn down."

Now that we have some background information, let's view a short video. To access the video, which we'll call Source 2, go to www.

EXPERT READER:

I know that videos incorporate audio and visuals to convey information. The visuals usually support the audio information. I'll need to listen carefully, since I also know that you can get a vast amount of information about a lot of different ideas very quickly in a video. I may need to watch the video several times in order to decide what is important to know vs. what is interesting.

dailymotion.com and search "Great Chicago Fire." Then select the video entitled "Wind Fuels Great Chicago Fire" (2:05). A good strategy for using short video clips is to first view the clip in its entirety to get the gist. Then, view it a second (and perhaps a third) time while thinking about what is important vs. what is interesting. Use the pause feature and jot down notes as you work through it. You'll see how the expert reader used the pause feature to capture important information that helps build knowledge of this event.

EXPERT READER:

√ I notice this video comes from a reliable source and that meteorologists and historians provide reliable information. √ At the 00:12 mark, I learn there was a high wind alert. Winds can cause erratic fire behavior. √ At 00:30, Mrs. O'Leary's cow is blamed for starting the fire. √ At 1:05, I learn there was a complicated process for notifying firefighters of fires in 1871. √ At 1:31, fire spread through whole block in twenty minutes; that's fast. √ At 1:56, buildings weren't tall, but there were a lot of them. This was a really hot fire that traveled fast

How did viewing this short video clip add to your understanding of the Great Chicago Fire? See how the expert reader uses this graphic organizer to collect important information gained from the text and the video.

Text	Video
• October 1871, Chicago	• Weather (wind) contributed to speed of fire
• One of the most destructive fires ever	• Started in the O'Learys' barn; cow?
• 18,000 buildings destroyed	• Complicated process to notify firefighters contributed to slow fire response
• 90,000 people homeless	• Fast moving; 20 minutes whole block
• City "just waiting to burn down"	• Lots of buildings that burned easily

Expert Reader Reflection

After evaluating this video clip, my knowledge of this disaster has increased. I now know that weather, human error, and the close proximity of the buildings contributed to the destruction caused by the fire. If I were to prepare a summary now on what I know, it would include additional details based on my integration of knowledge and evaluation of the video.

Let's see how the expert reader tackles a short-answer question that shows his skill at evaluating Sources 1 and 2.

Question: What are the advantages of Source 1 (text only)? What are the advantages of **Source 2** (video)?

Expert Reader: Text-only sources can include many descriptive details and creative language use. However, the reader has to create visual images in her mind to match the words on the page. This might be difficult if the text is about something she doesn't have background knowledge on. Videos, like Source 2, provide images to support the audio and are usually very engaging. The images can also quickly show us things we are not familiar with, like the process that was used to report fires in 1871. Videos can give us a lot of important information in a very short time.

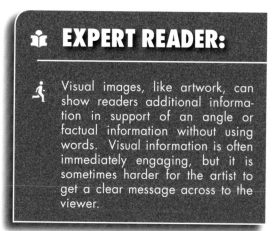

EXPERT READER:

Visual images, like artwork, can show readers additional information in support of an angle or factual information without using words. Visual information is often immediately engaging, but it is sometimes harder for the artist to get a clear message across to the viewer.

Next, let's take a look at two pieces of artwork that were made during the time period of the Great Chicago Fire. By analyzing and evaluating the artwork, we'll be able to add to our understanding of this tragedy.

Source 3

Chicago in Flames, Union Publishing Company, Lithograph, 1872.

PUBLISHED BY CURRIER & IVES   125 NASSAU ST NEW YORK.

Why did the artist choose this perspective?

How does viewing this artwork build your understanding?

Notice the coloring the artist chose.

The fire that destroyed much of Chicago's central business district was aided by the city's predominant use of wood for building materials, a drought prior to the fire, and strong winds.

📖 EXPERT READER:

√ I see how close the buildings are and how consuming the fire is. When buildings are close together, they burn quickly. √ The colors used give me the sense of the heat that must have been generated. I can tell this fire incinerated everything in its path. √ The perspective helps me grasp the magnitude of the fire and the enormous amount of people affected.

Now let's take a look at a second piece of artwork showing the fire from a different perspective.

Source 4

Why did the artist choose this perspective?
How does viewing this artwork build your understanding?
Notice the coloring the artist used.

⚜ EXPERT READER:

√ The artist chose to show the fire from street level so that we can see the masses of people, rich and poor, fleeing from the fire. √ The black-and-white coloring helps me understand the bleakness of the situation. √ This art is more personal. I can see people's faces as they carry what meager possessions they were able to save. I can feel their panic as the fire nipped at the heels of those who ran from it.

Ninety thousand people were left homeless following the Great Chicago Fire of 1871.

Follow along as the Expert Reader compares, contrasts, and evaluates Sources 3 and 4.

Source 3	Source 4
• **Coloring:** Beige, yellow, red, gray—beige to yellow to red gives a sense of the heat of fire	• **Coloring:** Black and white—creates feeling of bleakness while still conveying the idea of heat
• **Mood:** Tragic, but from a distance	• **Mood:** Tragic, up close
• **Perspective:** View from a distance	• **Perspective:** Street level
• How the city and its people were affected	• How individuals from all walks of life affected
• **Feel:** Catastrophic and affecting the city as a whole	• **Feel:** Personal and panicked

🔖 EXPERT READER:

 Both pieces of artwork are powerful; one helps me see the scope of the destruction, while the other helps me think about the people themselves who were caught in this awful situation and all they lost.

Expert Reader Reflection

My knowledge of the Great Chicago Fire is growing. I now have information about the fire itself and its causes, as well as how the people of the city were personally affected.

Again, let's pause to see how the expert reader tackles a short-answer question that shows her skill at evaluating Sources 3 and 4 as she integrates new knowledge with what she already knows.

Question: What can you learn about the Great Chicago Fire from Source 4 that you cannot learn from Source 3?

Expert Reader: Source 4 puts a personal face on the tragedy that Source 3 is not able to provide. Source 3 shows me the extent of the fire, while Source 4 shows me the people affected. While I learned in Source 1 that ninety thousand people were left homeless, Source 4 gave me faces to go with that number. I can see from the artwork the fear the people of Chicago felt as they were pursued by this fast-moving fire. I can see that they were able to save little, if anything, as they ran for their lives. I am beginning to wonder how they began rebuilding their lives and the city after this disaster.

EXPERT READER:

I know that maps are used to depict ideas in a location-based context. Maps can be used to reinforce ideas expressed in the text, so I'll need to pay attention to the area and content featured and if there's an underlying message.

Finally, let's take a moment to compare and contrast two maps, the first of which is static, or unmoving.

Source 5

Map showing the burned district in Chicago. The second map is an interactive pre-fire Chicago map. To

MAP SHOWING THE BURNT DISTRICT IN CHICAGO,

Published for the benefit of the Relief Fund by
3.ᴰ EDITION. THE R.P. STUDLEY COMPANY, ST. LOUIS.

How can a reader use this map to build knowledge?
What does this map show the reader?

EXPERT READER:

√ This map shows the reader the actual, physical land that was burned by the fire. You can see streets, blocks, and waterways. If you wanted, you could actually count up the blocks of the city that were destroyed. √ The reader can use this map to see the enormity of the disaster.

access the interactive map, which we'll call Source 6, go to www .greatchicagofire.org and search "Bird's Eye View of Pre-Fire Chicago." The map you are looking for will be the first image you see on the left side of the text. Be sure to use the zoom tool when exploring this map.

The expert reader now tackles a short-answer question that shows her skill at evaluating Sources 5 and 6 as she integrates new knowledge and understanding.

EXPERT READER:

I know that interactive multimedia usually involves movement and that in order to get the full effect of this media, I need to come together with the information in some way.

√ The interactive map is quite amazing. By using the zoom tool, I can actually see that someone drew in sketches of homes, churches, buildings, farms, etc., that existed before the fire. √ I can imagine the people who lived and worked in those buildings and all that might have been contained in each building.

Question: How can Sources 5 and 6 add to your understanding of the Great Chicago Fire?

Expert Reader: After viewing Sources 5 and 6, I can get a true feel of the extent of loss that the people of Chicago suffered. Source 5 shows the sheer magnitude of the area destroyed by the fire. Through the interactiveness of Source 6, I can actually see the individual buildings destroyed and get a feeling of the personal loss that was experienced by those who lived or had businesses there.

At this point, it makes sense to synthesize what we've learned about the Great Chicago Fire of 1871 from text and multiple multimedia sources and reflect on this experience.

Expert Reader's Final Thoughts on Multimedia Experience

I've learned much about this devastating fire by integrating and evaluating text and multimedia sources. I know when and where the fire occurred, and I also have an understanding about the causes of the fire and why it was so difficult to get under control. I understand the magnitude of this disaster and the destruction it left in its wake. With this knowledge comes new questions, however, such as could this fire have been avoided? How did the ninety thousand displaced people survive following the fire? How long did it take to rebuild the destroyed area of the city? Did the people who rebuilt the city learn from the mistakes that lead to the fire? If so, what did they do differently? Did other cities learn from the Chicago fire and build their cities differently?

I'm not sure I would have had these same questions if I were to have just read the text. One benefit of learning about topics using text and multimedia seems to be the direct-inquiry research opportunities that come from integrating and evaluating multiple sources to get a complete picture of a topic.

Conclusion

How well do you feel you've grasped the expert reader's use of tips and tricks for evaluating multimedia content? Decide if you're ready to move on to the guided practice in the next chapter or if you would like to take another pass through the expert reader's model.

CHAPTER 5

EVALUATING MULTIMEDIA CONTENT AND INFORMATIONAL TEXT: GUIDED PRACTICE

Now it's time for you to practice applying the tips and tricks as you integrate written text with multimedia sources to learn about the Japanese American internment during World War II. In addition to written text, you will be examining and evaluating a poster, a map, and a short video to build and strengthen your knowledge of this period of American history. Remember that each multimedia source has its own unique advantages and may help you create a solid foundation of understanding.

Since close reading the text is not the skill being practiced in this standard, the expert reader has prepared a summary of the text, which will help you comprehend the passage in a way that would closely duplicate your own close reading of it. You will want to read the passage and summary carefully before accessing the multimedia content. You will then use the practice prompts to guide you as you evaluate the multimedia sources, create graphic organizers to build knowledge on this topic, and answer short-response questions that demonstrate how to evaluate multimedia content. Check to see if your responses match possible responses provided.

Source 1

An Excerpt from
The Japanese American Internment
by Ann Heinrichs

It was a scene never before witnessed in the nation's history. More than 110,000 U.S. residents—men, women, and children of Japanese ancestry—were rounded up under military guard and sent to desolate camps surrounded by barbed wire fences. There they were interned, or imprisoned, from 1942–1945. These camps have variously been called relocation centers, internment camps, and concentration camps.

The Japanese American internment occurred at a time when fears about national security were running high. World War II (1939–1945) was in full force, with the United States at war both in Europe and in the Pacific region. As Japan was the major adversary in the Pacific, Japanese Americans along the Pacific Coast were viewed with suspicion. Did their loyalties lie with Japan, many Americans wondered, or with the United States? The U.S. Government decided that, for purposes of national security, people of Japanese ancestry should be confined under heavy guard until Japan was no longer a threat.

No citizens voted on the internment. Neither did their representatives in Congress, although Congress lent support to the measure. Instead, it was the result of a wartime proclamation issued by President Franklin D. Roosevelt. Still, public opinion largely supported the move, or at least accepted it as a wartime precaution.

The Japanese American internment raises some tough questions. Who was responsible for it, and how did it come about? Was it a necessary act of wartime, the result of wartime panic? How could other Americans, themselves the descendants of immigrant communities, stand by and watch this happen? Was the government justified in using ethnic identity as a reason for depriving people of their constitutionally guaranteed freedoms?

Expert Reader's Close Reading Summary

From 1942 to 1945, more than 110,000 American citizens with Japanese ancestry were imprisoned in internment camps by the U.S. government. The United States was involved in a conflict with Japan and because of this, the government decided that Japanese Americans should be kept under heavy guard until Japan was no longer a threat to America's national security. President Franklin D. Roosevelt made this decision, and most U.S. citizens accepted this internment as a necessary wartime precaution.

Now that you have some background information, let's take a look at a poster that one might have found in the San Francisco area during this time period and a map of the internment camps.

GUIDED PRACTICE PROMPT:

What do you know about using images, photography, and artwork to support and build understanding? Possible response: Visual images can show you additional information in support of an angle or give you additional factual information. Thinking about the artist's intent when this poster was made will help guide your understanding.

What do you know about maps that can help enhance your understanding? Possible response: Maps are often used to reinforce ideas contained in text and can be used to convey an underlying message. How can I use this map to fill in any gaps in my understanding?

Source 2
Instructions to All Persons of Japanese Ancestry
National Park Service, U.S. Department of the Interior Archives,

No Japanese person living in the above area will be permitted to change residence after 12 o'clock noon, P. W. T., Sunday, May 3, 1942, without obtaining special permission from the representative of the Commanding General, Northern California Sector, at the Civil Control Station located at:
920 "C" Street,
Hayward, California.

Such permits will only be granted for the purpose of uniting members of a family, or in cases of grave emergency.

The Civil Control Station is equipped to assist the Japanese population affected by this evacuation in the following ways:

1. Give advice and instructions on the evacuation.

2. Provide services with respect to the management, leasing, sale, storage or other disposition of most kinds of property, such as real estate, business and professional equipment, household goods, boats, automobiles and livestock.

3. Provide temporary residence elsewhere for all Japanese in family groups.

4. Transport persons and a limited amount of clothing and equipment to their new residence.

What do you think the poster author's point of view was on Japanese Americans? How can you tell?
Notice the date of this poster and the reporting date. What do you notice about the instructions?

On February 19, 1942, President Franklin D. Roosevelt issued Executive Order 9066, which permitted the deportation of Japanese Americans to internment camps.

 GUIDED PRACTICE PROMPT:

How can an evaluation of this poster enhance your understanding? Possible response:
√ The author of this poster most likely felt Japanese Americans were not true American citizens because he/she never refers to them as American, just "Japanese" or "persons."
√ Japanese Americans were given only a few days to prepare to leave their homes and lives. They could only bring what they could carry. There was no guarantee anything left behind would be safe.

 What are you thinking? Possible response: Did these citizens have any advance warning that this might happen or was this a surprise? They must have been frightened. Was there any other option for them than to go to the camps?

Source 3
Map of Japanese American Internment Camps
National Park Service, U.S. Department of the Interior Archives, Public Domain

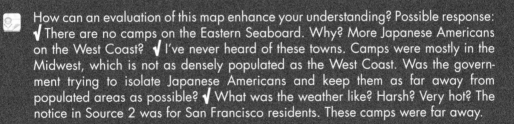

GUIDED PRACTICE PROMPT:

How can an evaluation of this map enhance your understanding? Possible response: √ There are no camps on the Eastern Seaboard. Why? More Japanese Americans on the West Coast? √ I've never heard of these towns. Camps were mostly in the Midwest, which is not as densely populated as the West Coast. Was the government trying to isolate Japanese Americans and keep them as far away from populated areas as possible? √ What was the weather like? Harsh? Very hot? The notice in Source 2 was for San Francisco residents. These camps were far away.

How did evaluating the poster and map add to your understanding of the Japanese American internment? Now, use a graphic organizer to collect important information gained from the text, poster, and map. See if your entries agree with some of the expert reader's entries featured below.

Possible Response for Graphic Organizer:

Text	Poster	Map
• U.S. in conflict with Japan during WWII	• Not treated as other U.S. citizens were	• Sent to camps far from home
• Japanese American citizens were imprisoned	• Little notice before they were made to leave lives	• Isolated locations, mostly in Midwest
• There were Questions about Japanese Americans' loyalty to the United States	• Bring only what could be carried	• No camps on East Coast
	• No guarantee belongings left behind would be safe until they returned	• Possibly harsh weather

Try reflecting on your multimedia experience by responding to the following short-answer question. Talk your answer through or jot it down on a separate piece of paper and then check your response against the possible response.

Question: What can you learn about the Japanese American internment from Sources 2 and 3 that you cannot learn from Source 1?

Possible Response: After evaluating Sources 2 and 3, I was able to integrate new knowledge into my understanding of this period in history. I learned Japanese American citizens were given very little notice before they were expected to leave their homes and businesses with only what they could carry. They were given no guarantee that belongings left behind would be safe until their return. They were sent to remote, isolated Midwestern locations far from their homes, where weather conditions may have been quite harsh. Japanese Americans were not treated as most Americans would expect to be treated. Instead, they were treated as if they were guilty of a crime. 🗨

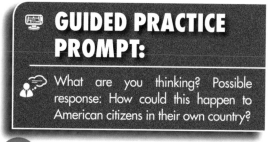

GUIDED PRACTICE PROMPT:

What are you thinking? Possible response: How could this happen to American citizens in their own country?

Finally, let's take a moment to view a short video clip. To access the video, which we'll call Source 4, go to www.history.com/site-map and search for "Japanese American Internment video." View the clip called "Japanese-American Relocation-World War II" (2:48). As you view and listen, jot down important information that adds to your knowledge. After you've evaluated the video clip, check your important facts against the possible responses.

Let's try one final short-response question that will allow you to reflect on your ability to integrate and evaluate information using multimedia sources. Talk your answer through or jot it down on a separate piece of paper and then check your response against the possible response.

GUIDED PRACTICE PROMPT:

What do you know about video renderings to support and build understanding? Possible response: I'll need to watch the clip in its entirety first and then once or twice more while using the pause feature to aid me as I take notes. I'll need to listen carefully as important ideas are conveyed quickly. Visual images will further support my understanding.

How can an evaluation of this video clip enhance your understanding? Possible response: √ Video comes from a reliable source. √ 00:11 Internment began two months after Pearl Harbor. √ 00:40 Farmers had to leave their farms untended. √ 00:58–1:08 Notice barren landscape. √ 1:13 Japanese American soldiers serving in WWII while families were in camps. √ 1:30 Barbed wire, watchtowers, sentry guards, minimal rations, curfew; like jail. √ 2:17 Attitude of pride when able to return. √ 2:38 Many find everything they owned in ruins. √ 2:41 $1.6 billion in reparations in 1988 (forty years later).

Question: How does Source 4 add to your understanding of the Japanese American internment?

Possible Response: After evaluating the content of the video clip, I was able to determine the reason for the government's actions. If I'm not familiar with the bombing of Pearl Harbor, I'll want to do some further research. I learned that Japanese American soldiers were serving their country in World War II while many of their families were being held in the internment camps. I would have been so angry, but it seems like many soldiers chose a different attitude; one of pride in their ancestry and loyalty to the United States. The video clip did confirm my feeling that the internment camps were like a jail; there were barbed wire, watchtowers, sentries with guns, minimal rations, and a curfew. Basic American freedoms were taken away from the Japanese Americans in these camps. I learned that when they were released from these camps, many found nothing left of the lives they had before. That must have been heartbreaking and difficult. It doesn't appear that the U.S. government provided financial, rebuilding help to the people it imprisoned until forty years later. That seems shameful to me and might be something I would want to research further.

Final Thoughts on This Multimedia Experience

At this point, you probably have more questions about the Japanese American internment than you have answers for. That's one of the benefits of evaluating multimedia sources—it frequently leads you to research questions that you are genuinely interested in learning the answers to. Jot down a few of your most pressing questions about this period of U.S. history and see if you can find some answers using the multimedia tips and tricks you have been practicing. Keep in mind that your school library media specialist is an excellent resource to help you with multimedia content and research.

A New Expert Reader!

Now that you've mastered how to use tips and tricks for evaluating multimedia content, you're on your way to becoming an expert reader! Continue to practice with different types of multimedia sources. You'll see that your attempts to grapple with classroom and assigned texts are far easier now.

APOSTROPHE A poetry term referring to a speaker calling out to someone (or an idea or object) who is not actually there.

ARTWORK Illustrations, photographs, or other non-textual material.

AUDIO Sound, especially when recorded, transmitted, or reproduced.

CARTOON A simple drawing showing the features of its subjects in a humorously exaggerated way.

CLOSE READING The deep, analytical reading of a brief passage of text in which the reader constructs meaning based on author intention and text evidence.

DIAGRAM A simplified drawing showing the appearance, structure, or workings of something; a schematic representation.

EVALUATE To appraise or assess.

IMAGE A representation of the external form of a person or thing in art.

INFORMATIONAL TEXT A type of nonfiction text, such as an article; essay; opinion piece; memoir; or historical, scientific, technical, or economic account that is written to give facts or inform about a topic.

INTEGRATE To join together with or combine.

INTERACTIVE MEDIA The integration of digital media, including combinations of electronic text, graphics, moving images, and sound, that allows a person to interact with data.

LITERATURE Imaginary writing, such as poetry, mysteries, myths, creation stories, science fiction, allegories, and other genres, that tells a story.

MAP A diagrammatic representation of an area of land or sea showing physical features, cities, roads, etc.

MULTIMEDIA Using or involving several forms of communication or expression.

PERSONIFICATION The attribution of a personal nature or human characteristics to something nonhuman.

PERSPECTIVE The position that is taken by someone.

PHOTOGRAPHY The art or practice of taking and processing photographs.

PITCH The degree of highness or lowness of a tone.

POETIC INVERSION An inversion of the normal grammatical word order; it may range from a single word moved from its usual place to a pair of words inverted or to even more extremes.

POSTER A large, usually printed placard, bill, or announcement.

SIMILE A figure of speech involving the comparison of one thing with another thing of a different kind, used to make a description more emphatic or vivid.

TONE The writer's or artist's communication of an overall feeling or attitude about a subject.

TOPIC The subject of a piece of text or multimedia source.

VANTAGE POINT A place or position affording a good view of something.

VIDEO The recording, reproducing, or broadcasting of moving visual images.

FOR MORE INFORMATION

Council of Chief State School Officers (CSSO)
One Massachusetts Avenue NW, Suite 700
Washington, DC 20001-1431
(202) 336-7000
Website: http://www.ccsso.org
The Common Core State Standards Initiative is a state-led effort coordinated
by the National Governors Association Center for Best Practices (NGA
Center) and the Council of Chief State School Officers (CCSSO). The
standards provide a clear and consistent framework to prepare students
for college and the workforce.

National Governors Association (NGA)
Hall of the States
444 North Capitol Street, Suite 267
Washington, DC 20001-1512
(202) 624-5300
Website: http://www.nga.org
The National Governors Association and the Council of Chief State School
Officers go together—both organizations were responsible for the creation
of the Common Core State Standards so they share the description provided.

National Parent Teacher Association (PTA)
12250 North Pitt Street
Alexandria, VA 22314
(703) 518-1200
Website: http://www.pta.org
The National PTA enthusiastically supports the adoption and implementation
by all states of the Common Core State Standards. The standards form a
solid foundation for high-quality education.

New York State Education Department
89 Washington Avenue
Albany, NY 12234
(518) 474-3852
Website: http://www.engageny.org
EngageNY.org is developed and maintained by the New York State Education
    Department. This is the official website for current materials and
    resources related to the implementation of the New York State P–12
    Common Core Learning Standards (CCLS).

Partnership for Assessment of Readiness for College and Careers
1400 16th Street NW, Suite 510
Washington, DC 20036
(202) 745-2311
Website: http://www.parcconline.org
The Partnership for Assessment of Readiness for College and Careers
    (PARCC) is a consortium of eighteen states, plus the District of Columbia
    and the U.S. Virgin Islands, working together to develop a common set of
    K–12 assessments in English and math anchored in what it takes to be
    ready for college and careers.

U.S. Department of Education
Department of Education Building
400 Maryland Avenue SW
Washington, DC 20202
(800) 872-5327
Website: http://www.edu.gov
Nearly every state has now adopted the Common Core State Standards.
    The federal government has supported this state-led effort by helping
    to ensure that higher standards are being implemented for all students

and that educators are being supported in transitioning to new standards.

Websites

Due to the changing nature of Internet links, Rosen Publishing has developed an online list of websites related to the subject of this book. This site is updated regularly. Please use this link to access the list:

http://www.rosenlinks.com/CCRGR/Multi

Baum, L. Frank. *The Wonderful Wizard of Oz*. Chicago, IL: The George M. Hill Company, 1900.

Beers, Kylene, and Robert E. Probst. *Notice & Note: Strategies for Close Reading*. Portsmouth, NH: Heinemann, 2013.

Chicago Historical Society. "The Great Chicago Fire and the Web of Memory." Retrieved February 14, 2014 (http://www.greatchicagofire.org).

Dailymotion. Retrieved February 13, 2014 (http://www.dailymotion.com).

Fountas, Irene C., and Gay Su Pinnell. *Genre Study: Teaching with Fiction and Nonfiction Books*. Portsmouth, NH: Heinemann, 2012.

Heinrichs, Ann. *Japanese American Internment*. Pelham, NY: Benchmark, 2010.

History. Retrieved February 17, 2014 (http://www.history.com).

Librivox. Retrieved February 13, 2014 (https://librivox.org).

Marx, Christy. *The Great Chicago Fire of 1871*. New York, NY: Rosen Publishing Group, 2004.

National Park Service, U.S. Department of the Interior Archives. "History of Japanese American Internment." Retrieved February 16, 2014 (http://www.nps.gov).

Whitman, W. "*O Captain! My Captain!*" *Leaves of Grass*. 1855. Public domain.

Wordsworth, W. "I Wandered Lonely Like a Cloud (Daffodils)." *Poems in Two Volumes*. 1807. Public domain.

About the Authors

Sandra K. Athans is a national board–certified practicing classroom teacher with fifteen years of experience teaching reading and writing at the elementary level. She is the author of several teacher-practitioner books on literacy including *Quality Comprehension* and *Fun-tastic Activities for Differentiating Comprehension Instruction*, both published by the International Reading Association. Athans has presented her research at the International Reading Association, the National Council of Teachers of English Conferences, and New York State Reading Association conferences. Her contributions have appeared in well-known literacy works including *The Literacy Leadership Handbook* and *Strategic Writing Mini-Lessons*. She is also a children's book writer and specializes in high-interest, photo-informational books published with Millbrook Press, a division of Lerner Publishing Group.

Athans earned a B.A. in English from the University of Michigan, an M.A. in elementary education from Manhattanville College, and an M.S. in literacy (birth–grade 6) from Le Moyne College. She is also certified to teach secondary English. In addition to teaching in the classroom, she is an adjunct professor at Le Moyne College and provides instruction in graduate-level literacy classes. This spring, she was awarded Outstanding Elementary Social Studies Educator by the Central New York Council for the Social Studies. She serves on various ELA leadership networks and collaborates with educators nationwide to address the challenges of the Common Core Standards. The Tips and Tricks series is among several Common Core resources she has authored for Rosen Publishing.

Robin W. Parente is a practicing reading specialist and classroom teacher with over fifteen years of experience teaching reading and writing at the elementary level. She also serves as the elementary ELA coordinator for a medium-sized district in central New York, working with classroom teachers to implement best literacy practices in the classroom. Parente earned a B.S. in elementary education and a M.S. in education/literacy from the State University of New York, College at Oswego. She is a certified reading specialist (PK–12) and elementary classroom teacher and has served on various ELA leadership networks to collaborate with educators to address the challenges of the Common Core Standards. The Tips and Tricks series is among several Common Core resources she has authored for Rosen Publishing.

Photo Credits

Cover © iStockphoto.com/Andrew Rich; pp. 4–5 © iStockphoto.com/skynesher; p. 9 © Michael McGarty; pp. 15, 32, 36, 41, 42 Library of Congress Prints and Photographs Division; p. 20 Buyenlarge/SuperStock; p. 26 Popperfoto/Getty Images; p. 44 Chicago History Museum/Archive Photos/Getty Images; 50 Courtesy National Archives, photo 210-G-A561; p. 51 Globe Turner/Shutterstock.com; icons © iStockphoto.com/sodafish, © iStockphoto.com/nipponsan, © iStockphoto.com/tarras79, © iStockphoto/Aaltazar, © iStockphoto/Alex Belominsky.

Designer: Nicole Russo; Editor: Bethany Bryan;
Photo Researcher: Cindy Reiman